MUDDY SNEAKERS and OTHER FAMILY HASSLES

MUDDY SNEAKERS and OTHER FAMILY HASSLES

IRENE BURK HARRELL

and

Tommy, Alice, Dino, Susan, 'Guerite, and Maria

ABINGDON PRESS

Nashville   *New York*

Copyright © 1973, 1974 by Abingdon Press

All rights reserved.
No part of this book may be reproduced in any manner whatsoever without written permission of the publisher except brief quotations embodied in critical articles or reviews. For information address Abingdon Press, Nashville, Tennessee.

Library of Congress Cataloging in Publication Data:

HARRELL, IRENE BURK.
  Muddy sneakers and other family hassles.
  1. Family—Prayer-books and devotions—English.
I. Title.
BV255.H34   242   73-15575

ISBN 0-687-27295-5

to the kids
    naturally—
        yours and ours—
            God bless 'em

PREFACE

There's always been
  a generation gap
We used to think
  it was an unbridgeable chasm
    an impossibility of communication
    a morass of misunderstanding
      between the old and young
        especially between parents and their
          progeny
And we fretted at its frustrations
  lamented its limitations
  wished it would swallow itself
    vanish into its own abyss
And we tried techniques
But they didn't help
The gap kept on gapping
  kids on one side
  grown-ups on the other
  chasm between
    uncrossable, insatiable, defiant
Well, it took a long time
  half of almost forever
But God finally got through
  our impenetrable denseness
    (with him, all things are possible)
And the substance of his getting through was this:
"My children
  the generation gap
    isn't between you and your children
      between you and your parents
      between you and any other people
        half or twice your age
  The generation gap is within you
    where heaven is supposed to be
  But you can't have heaven
    until you're born again
      re-generated

        trusting my Son for everything
The generation gap
  is the space between
    what you are
      and
    what I have given you power to become
      as sons of God
When you have grown up
  into the stature of my Son
    there will be no gap
      within you
      among you
    You will be one in him"
And so
  when we and our children
  when we and our parents
  when we and any other people
    can't get through to each other
  we pray in Jesus' name
    and he becomes our bridge
    he becomes the Way
    he gets through to them
    and he gets through to us
It is our prayer
  that the tracks of *Muddy Sneakers*
    will point you
      in the same direction

CONTENTS

City Dump 11
Hurry Up and Wait 15
The Long Hair Hassle 19
Listless? Not Us 20
A Special Child 23
The Case of the Unmuddied Sneakers 25
Varieties of Intelligence 28
The Man with the Hoe 30
On Appetites 33
The Sun Shines Bright
   —Even When It's Cloudy 35
Helping 37
Whistler's Mother a Cop-Out? 40
Ancestor Worship? 42
Is Fairness an Obsolete Word? 46
Special Privileges 51
The Dating Game 53
Higher Education 57
Fragile—Handle with Care 60
Fat Head 62
Signs of Spring 64
On Neck-Wringing 66
Helpmeet 70
Driver's License Dread 71
Report Card Reporting 72
Sunny Side Up? 78
Surprised by Joy 83
Conclusion Leaping with
   Trap Running 85
Off 87
The Living End—As a New Beginning 92
Reading Glasses 96
If There Be Anything Lovely,
   Think About It 98
Slowpoke 101
Servant Service 105

CITY DUMP

Lord
  I'm orbiting—
    numb
    absolutely numb
that my sweet-sixteen
  would rocket off
    into such a tirade
at MY unreasonableness
  for gently suggesting
    that she hang up her clothes
      left lying in the heap
      cascaded from her suitcase
        over a week ago
It baffles me
  Lord
I'm out of control
  weightlessly adrift
  at her inability to acknowledge
    the RES IPSA LOQUITUR reasons
    WHY
      her clothes should be
        hung up
          or
        folded away
        instead of left

                r
              p e
                  c
           g   a
        n   r
      i   i
     r   o
    e   u
   w   s
  o   l
t   y

in a volcanic mass
   sporadically erupting
      from the room's only
         comfortable chair
She keeps wanting me
  to tell her WHY
    Lord
You know I don't have
  any whys
    satisfactory to her—
That the clothes
  need to be
    ready for wearing
isn't a reason
  she buys
nor neatness for its own sake
nor for the sake
  of finding things
    when she's in a hurry
She thinks I should avert my eyes
  when I chance past her door
    not to be staggered by
      the eloquent evidence
        of earthquake there
Lord, I'm not the only mother
  who's wondered
  who's failed to comprehend
    the necessity for
      supercolossal
        cataclysmic
          catastrophic
        disaster areas
          in kids' rooms
What's the answer
  Lord?

Lord
  you know I don't like
    having my room look
      like a tornado just went through it
        any more than she does
But I've been busy
And which is more important:
  having a neat sanitation-grade-A room
  or being a friend
    the kind who writes letters to somebody
    the kind who plays tennis with somebody
    the kind who's not too busy
      to let somebody cry on her shoulder?
And by the way, Lord
  the clothes haven't been there a week yet
    just a few days
They were getting back in circulation, too
  gradually
Every time I needed something
  I'd haul it out and wear it
    and put it in the dirty clothes basket
      when I took it off
It'd all reach the closet eventually
And they weren't towering precariously
Why, I don't have enough clothes to make a pile
  sufficiently towering
    to be threatening to anything
      except a curious puppy maybe
And we keep the door closed
  so curious puppies
  and marauding little people
    can't wander in
No one has to go in our room
  except me, my sister, and our friends
    And if they're really friends
      they'll love me in spite of my sloppiness

       and maybe offer to help clean it up
and it'd be easy for Mama to steer clear
  of chancing past my doorway altogether
    It's at the far end of the hall
All that Mama's over-and-over mentioning
  ever does
    is make me mad

                                            r
                                         e
                                  w
                              o
    more inclined to let the tower t
        for half of forever
But really, Lord
  any fool can see that it does need cleaning up
    (just because my room looks like a pigpen
    doesn't mean I have pigs' brains)
      but I prefer to be neat on my own accord
And since Mama hasn't bothered me about it
  for a few hours
    I think I'll go exercise my own accord
      and move the mountain

HURRY UP AND WAIT

But, Mama,
  I've gotta have the scrapbook TONIGHT
  so I can start workin' on my project

How many times
  over the years
  I've heard—and heeded—
    urgent requests like that
      and gone traipsing out
        in the rainswept dark
          to slosh around uptown
        tracking down elusive cardboard
          or poster paper
          or notebooks just the right size
          or scrapbooks just the right texture
        hours after
          the logical supply stores
            have logically battened their hatches
              for the night
and then
  weeks later
    on the day of the deadline
    or late the night before
  I've heard the suspicious rattly crinkle
    of cellophane being unwrapped
      from the pristine, untouched-till-then
        scrapbook, notebook, posterboard
          or whatever
and THEN
  he wants permission
    to burn the midnight oil

You HAVE to let me stay up late
  Mom
The project's due tomorrow!

He glares at me

like he's wondering
>   *How stupid can you get?*

And we all get busy
  helping
    hurrying
      holding our breaths
  fetching this and that
    scissoring pictures
    lettering posters
    or whomping up glops of papier-mâché
  looking up leaf identifications
    taping botanical specimens to a page
    typing a last-minute imperfect report
  and fussing about how he should've begun
    soon enough
      to do everything properly himself
By breakfast the next morning
  we're all still laboring
    the project still unfinished
and I phone the carpool
  "Don't come for our boy
  we'll bring him along later"
And we do
I harbor a dismal hunch
  that his project is a flop
  that he's sure to flunk
and I try to swallow a certainty
  that my project
    bringing up a boy in the way he should go
  has flopped too
  that I've flunked as a mother
Lord
  how CAN I get him
    to be more responsible?

Dear God
  it's so easy to put work-things off
    and decide that now is the time
      to play football
      or just go fishing
  I can always do my project later
    It's not due for a month
Only then I forget all about it
  until the night before it's due
And I get in a frenzy to begin
  when I should be finishing up
I wish I HAD started a month ago
  like I meant to
so mine could have been
  the best in the class
instead of just squeaking by
At breakfast time
  a visitor would think
    we were all on a diet of leaves
      The table's knee-deep in 'em
But I'm finally finished
  and get to school
    with the minimum fifty leaves
      in my book
I put it on the teacher's desk
  and go to my seat
    feeling a little bit proud of myself
      to have accomplished the clearly impossible
But then I start to think
  Didn't my teacher say
    to include our name
      or else he would drop our grade
        one whole letter?
And didn't he state

that he required
  a table of contents
    and the scientific names
      as well as the common ones?
I'm afraid he did
  but it's too late now
    I guess I won't make a very good grade after all
God
  answer Mama's prayer
    Make me more responsible

THE LONG HAIR HASSLE

About long hair, Lord
Both of our boys have it
  becomingly
    I think
      (now that I've gotten used to it)
I just wonder
  Would long hair have become beautiful sooner
    if I hadn't looked at it
      in the beginning
    with such a long face?
Truly
  you keep on making
    everything beautiful in its time
Thank you, Lord
  that there has come the time
    when even I
      can see
      the beautiful

LISTLESS? NOT US

Lord
  you know
    we're kind of a listing family
      I think
Probably comes of having
  lots of interesting things to do
So
  there's usually a growing grocery list
    magneted to the refrigerator
  an office supply list
    stuck under the corner of my desk blotter
  and other lists
    of things to do
    places to go
    people to call
here and there
  all over the place
Lists seem to suit us
  give us confidence
    we won't forget
      something vital
  and a sense of achievement
    when everything's crossed off
      accomplished
I love especially
  the lists our children make
Last week
  I came across an old one
      Dino had prepared
        before a camping trip
          a couple of years ago
There was an understandable section
  labeled
    First Aid Stuff
  with things a Scout might need
    to be prepared for

    sunburn
    snakebite
    blisters
    mosquito bites
    and smelly feet
  nothing especially interesting or revelatory
    about that
and the section of the list entitled
  Things I Need to Get
    could have been anybody's
But the other part of the list
  hit me where I live
    not because of what was on it
      (ordinary mundane things
        not to be forgotten
          shoes
          and pants
          and how many pair
            of underwear)
  but because of what he called it:
    not "Things I Need to Take"
  but
    Things I Need to Find
Lord
  how betraying
  how revealing
Truly
  what is hidden
    shall be shouted from the housetops
Finding things
  is so often the biggest problem
    around here
  the cause of most frustrations
We don't lack what we need
  but we can't find it anywhere
Lord

is it that we have too many things
    to keep track of
or is it something deeper—
    that we blame someone else
        every time something's out of place
Lord
    will we have to keep on being disorderly
        as long as we insist
            that lostness is someone else's fault
                and not our own?
Lord
    make us so we can forgive
        and take the blame ourselves
            even when we don't deserve it
Lord
    let us get our forgiveness in order
        for your coming

A SPECIAL CHILD

Lord
  she's not my child exactly
  she was born to another family
    in our town
but we see her often
  and love her
To the world
  she's retarded
    someone who didn't quite
      come out right
    someone who can't cope
      as well as we do
    who doesn't grasp things
      as fast maybe
    or needs a different handle to take hold of
    or can't take hold at all
I've wondered about her, Lord
  how she fits in
    in your perfect scheme of things
There have been days
  when she came to set our table
    or love our little ones
    or share a bowl of fresh-cooked collards
      (her almost favorite dish)
  when you poured out so much
    of your love for her
      through me
  that I stood back amazed
and I began to see her
  through your eyes
and had no regret
  no sorrow at all
    that she was exactly as she is
And I understood
  how you could see her
    and say that it was good

I could say it too
  and wouldn't have changed her
    one iota
    not a single thing about her
Oh, Lord
  that's what love always does
    isn't it?
loves us completely
  exactly as we are
Love always sees us
  beautiful
    and perfect
      in the midst of our supposed imperfection
Lord
  thank you
    for this understanding
    that when we all come
      into a full measure of willingness
        to let your love flow through us
          there won't be any pitiful creatures
            any unlovely ones
              among us
          because
            in the twinkling of an eye
          your love
            will see them whole

THE CASE OF THE UNMUDDIED SNEAKERS

Dear God
  why do parents
    always think
      that they are right?
I took my dirty tennis shoes
  outdoors
  and wiped the dirt off
    on the grass
  because Mama doesn't want
    muddy things in the washing machine
And I brought them back
  and tossed them in the laundry room
    for her to wash
But when she saw them
  Wow

  Go clean your shoes off, Dino

When I told her
  I had done it already
    she looked at me
      with that exasperated look
        she gets sometimes
      and then she looked at the shoes
        like you'd examine an amoeba
          under a microscope
      and she finally found a spot
        where
          by trying real hard
          she managed to scrape up
            an infinitesimal bit
              of leftover mud
                with her thumbnail
and claimed
  I hadn't done
    a very good job
God

they weren't all that dirty
And I know she wasn't worried about
  clogging up the drain
    because she made me
     wash the shoes
       in the bathroom sink
         before she'd put them
        in the washer
About then
  is when
    Daddy walked in
     and told me off
When I tried to explain
  he interrupted and said
    he wasn't interested in my opinions
     just in my unquestioning obedience
      to Mama's instructions
Lord
  I get tired of it
Lord
  what's wrong with being right?

Being right's
  all right
isn't it, Lord?
Nothing wrong with
  being right
    at all
If all of us
  were always right
    in one another's eyes
would earth be heaven?
I'm not sure
Maybe it would just be
    sanctimonious
Ugh!

But I do know this:
The rightest thing
   that we can do
      is to love one another
         right or wrong
And I thank you, God
   that you keep on using
      even our mistakes
         to draw us closer to one another
            and to you
         in forgiveness
            and in love

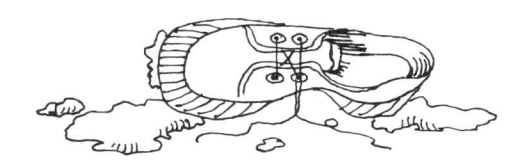

VARIETIES OF INTELLIGENCE

"I'm so thankful
  for all the things
    your son has fixed
      around our house"
I told my neighbor
"Why
  things that have been
    falling apart and aparter
      forever
    he's made as good as new"
And I told her about the screen door
  whose screen was tacked intact now
    where it had bulged and dangled
  about the swivel chair
    that had collapsed
    that sits upright
      and wheels easily to and fro
  about the valet
  with the broken back
    that can hang a shirt again
  about other things
    too numerous to name
She received my praise
  uneasily
  uncomfortably
and then explained
"I'm glad he's been some help
  but I don't understand—
    with so many men in your family
  why you don't have anyone
    who can fix anything"
I had to laugh
  comfortably
  easily

because it's true
    we're not much at
        making things new
But her whole family
  has skills
    with hammers and saws
    paint and glue
    needle and thread
My daughter said
  Mama, their family is the kind of smart
  that does somebody some good
The implication was
  that "our kind of smart"
    in letters or in law
      is PRACTICALLY worthless
But Lord
  we know
    that you're the one
      who made us different
And we rejoice in it
  that you need us all
      green-thumbs and all-thumbs
Thank you for showing me
  that it's true
    within a family too
That our differences
  and different ways of doing
    and different ways of looking at things
      —even our generation gaps—
    are not necessary nuisances
      but part of your more excellent way
        part of your purpose
          that we might grow up
            needing one another
            needing to love

THE MAN WITH THE HOE

Lord
  I was glad I was innocent
  when he came in asking
    who had had the hoe
It didn't sound like
  whoever had had it
    was in line for the medal of honor
      or anything like that
No, Lord
  it sounded like
    whoever had had it
      had *had* it!
Of course it came out
  that our number one son had used it
    to dig fishing worms
and not being designed for digging deep
  but for scratching the surface
    the hoe had broken in protest
I couldn't blame the hoe
  for that
But there was some blame
  for the number one son
    who had forgotten to mention
      the calamity
  and had gone off fishing
    leaving the hoe where it fell
And when his daddy needed it
  and came across it
    in the corner of the garden
      useless—
How many times have I told you . . . ?
Our question tells the answer
  doesn't it, Lord
    and I confess
      I ask it so often
Any time we've told them

    times without number
    times ad infinitum
       and it hasn't sunk in
    we've failed to teach them at all
Forgive me, Lord
   I know
      there's a world of difference
         between telling and teaching
Any teacher knows it
   and parents ought to know it too
What is there in us
   that makes us so obtuse?
Is it laziness
   that keeps us from following through
      from reinforcing a telling
      to make it teaching
         with practice under supervision
            with appropriate rewards and penalties
               for learning and not learning?
Or is it unforgiveness
   that makes us want to blame
      instead of intelligently to correct
         so the correcting will bear fruit?
Whatever we lack
   Lord
      of industry or love
   make up in us
      please
   that we might teach
And Lord
   I'm not sure
      whether there will be
         broken hoes
            in heaven or not
But if there are
   I know they won't make heaven

      less heavenly
         because our reaction to their discovery
            in heaven
         will always be
            pure, poured-out love
Lord
   let it be
      that way
         on earth
            as it is in heaven

ON APPETITES

The snack after breakfast
  the bite before supper
    the in-between munching
      that knows no end
Lord
  every mother knows
    that the way to tell
      when she's almost finished
        with the dishes
      is not to sight along the counter
        left and right
      to see what remains to be done
    but to be aware
      when the first kid comes in
        for a drink of water
        another glass of milk
        or a look in the refrigerator
          to see if there's anything left to eat
That's how we know
  when we're almost finished
When it begins again
  the stoking of stomachs
  the sating of appetites
    that makes for constant clutter
    and never-doneness in the kitchen
One day I asked
  Why can't you eat enough at mealtime?
The answer was loud and clear
  made perfect sense
Gee, Mom, I'm not hungry then

Eating
  feeding our families
    sweeping our floors
      washing our clothes
        picking things up—

They're never finished forever
They're part of the ongoing fabric
   of life
So be it
And Lord
   let there be
      in us
   that kind of an insatiableness
   a never-doneness
      in our seeking after you
Let us never get enough
Let there be no time
   when we're not hungry for more
Let that be
   warp and woof
      of our lives too
Partaking of living bread
   and water welling up
      to eternal life

THE SUN SHINES BRIGHT—
EVEN WHEN IT'S CLOUDY

Lord
  I didn't think it necessary
    to remind someone
      as old as he is
      as painfully experienced
        in the ways of sunshine
    to be lavish with the lotion
    and soon with a shirt
It didn't cross my mind
Permission to go to the beach
  was mine to give
How to take care of himself
  once he got there
    was his business
But, oh, Lord
  the agony of that awful burn
Pain was scrawled on his face that night
  when he didn't think I was looking
He brushed it off
  when I asked
    if he'd let me put something on it

Naw
  It's not so bad
  Be all right tomorrow
  I don't think it's even gonna blister

Yes
  it was all right tomorrow
  all right
He spent the day in bed
  too fried to move
  too sick for school
And it was all right
  the day after that
    and the day after that
      and the day after that

when all the fiery-furnaced skin
   began to hang in sheets
He was lucky, Lord
   and blessed
      not to be sicker than he was
         and
      to come out of his peeling
         in one piece
I'm grateful
   but how long will it be
      before he learns
         how much enough is enough
or will he ever?

*   *   *   *   *   *   *   *   *   *

Thank you, Lord
   for reminding me
      of the myriad things essential
         you've been trying to get through
            my thick head for years
And only now
   are my ears
      beginning to open
Thank you for trusting
   that with your infinite patience
      a little infinitely longer
   I will one day begin to act
      as if
         maybe
      I hear

HELPING

Lord
  you heard them

That sure was a good dinner
  Mom
Yeah
  I enjoyed it

They all said it
  or words to that effect
    and meant them
  shoving their chairs
    away from the table
  and patting their paunches
  to show how each had done his share
    of the enjoying
And they weren't just trying
  to be polite
It WAS a good dinner
  and not for company this time
    just for them
I'd worked all day on it
  kind of a thank you, Lord
    for the celebration I felt
      in my heart
    knowing they'd all be home
      together
I'd gone to the pleasureful bother
  of making biscuits from scratch
  stuffing a turkey
  making my own cranberry sauce
instead of serving mammon at my desk
  and taking them out to eat
Well
  it was interesting to see

how some settled down
> to read the paper
> to play the piano
> to take a walk
> to catch a nap
> to lean on a cupboard and talk
>> or just to toast in front of the fire
>
> each to some enjoyment
> blissfully unaware
>> (at least no guilty consciences
>>> resulting in helping hands)
>>
>> of the cleaning up that had to be done

So I
> who had already worked in the kitchen all day
>> began
>>> clearing the table
>>> putting away food
>>> washing the dishes
>>> drying them
>>> stacking them away

Well
> I didn't mind doing it

The whole day was dedicated to being
> a labor of love

but it did seem
> that someone ought to offer
>> to do more than VOICE appreciation
>
> they ought to show it
>> by helping

It's all my fault, of course
> for unintentionally
>> bringing them up to be that way

Lord
> I love to wait on them
>> mostly

but help them see
   what joy helping can bring
      to their hearts and mine
and to the wholeness
   of a family

WHISTLER'S MOTHER A COP-OUT?

Lord
  I just love
    being the mother
      of such a creative child
Her drawings
  never fail to thrill me
  with their preciousness
Her projects—and sculptures—
  tickle me pink
    with their utter originality
Originality
  you are the very soul
    of Susan
I glow with pride
  —my Susan—
and hang her pictures on the wall
But Father
  sometimes I wonder
    Does being creative
      HAVE to mean
        being such an absolute slop
          about her closet
          and her shelves
          and her drawers
          and even the middle of the floor?
(I won't even mention the conglomeration
  rendering the carport impassable)
It never seems to matter
  how many extra places I rig up
    for her to put things
      to keep them orderly
  or how diligently I labor
    to get it all cleaned out
      once and for all
  dispatching all the dust fuzzies
    the peanut butter cracker crumbs

             the wadded rumpled paper
             the multicolored mildewed socks
             the poster-painty washcloths
             the glue-laden popsickle sticks
        sorting all the heaped-up clothes
             giving them the eye and nose test
                  to figure out a fitting destination
                       laundry or closet or charity or junkheap
        organizing all the keepables
             into neatly labeled boxes
In less than two weeks' time
     it looks as if I'd never touched it
        the mingling is that advanced
             with pack-rat tendencies blossoming
                  in closets and drawers jammed with
                       sticky chewing gum wrappers
                       and empty toilet paper rolls
                       and half-sucked suckers
                       and undisposed-of disposable tissues
                            ragged with the need for disposition
                       and unemptied thermoses
                            of long-since sour
                                 sweet chocolate milk
                       and ten years' worth
                            of arithmetic test papers
"Aauugghh!"
     as Charlie Brown would say
I don't have my own word for it
     exactly
but Father
     it bugs me
Should it?

ANCESTOR WORSHIP?

Lord
  you know how much I want to go
    to Winston-Salem
      for the Governor's School reunion
I know that Thanksgiving
  is a family time
    but it's the only time we could arrange
      our get-together
    and we've been planning it ever since July
    much longer than Mama's been planning
      for us all to go to Grandma's
I'd love to see Grandma
  but not then
This might be my only chance to see
  those Governor's School kids again
Grandma will be around next year
  and many more to come
Besides
  the state championship football game
    will be played that weekend
    and if I'm in Winston
      I might be able to see it
        or at least hear it on the radio
There's no way I can hear it
  at Ohio Grandma's
It's important to me
  to see our team become state champs again
    the fourth time in five years
Just think how disappointed
  all my friends will be if I'm not there
They have a right to see me too
and I want to see them
Why
  Lord
why can't I go?

Governor's School, Lord
I almost cringe when I hear it
She's raised such a commotion
   about wanting to go to their reunion
      instead of to Grandma's
         with the rest of us
It's true I need her
   Lord
      in one of the cars
         to mother one of the little ones
It's a long ride
   impossible for the eight of us
      in ONE vehicle
and I'll need her at Grandma's too
   but that's not the basic reason why
      I want her to go our way
nor is it connected with the fact
   that the proposed reunion
      raises my eyebrows a little
The planned outing
   is an outright
      motel get-together
         of bright kids
      with no adult sponsors
         no grown-up chaperons
The Governor's School officials
   have written to parents already
      "We have nothing to do with it.
      For information, write a person called
         Peaches . . ."
Well, I'm sure it'll all be just peachy
(I lie—I don't know that at all)
   but I don't have to hang my demurrer on that
Lord
   there's something in a man
      or a woman

especially a father or a mother
    and even more especially a grandfather
that craves occasional completeness
that wants all that belongs to him
    all that comes from his loins
to be together sometimes
    without exception
I sense my father feels it now
"All six of the kids
  and all their kids
    had Thanksgiving with us this year," he'll say
"except Martha and her gang
  and we telephoned them
in Germany where her husband's stationed
Yes," he'll say, and he'll remember the day
    fondly forever
"We were all together except Martha and her gang
    for Thanksgiving in '71"
Lord
  I want it to be like that
    for him to remember
  and not gum it up with a messy
"—well, actually, Alice wasn't there either.
  She's Irene's oldest daughter, you know.
  Something about a reunion with some kids
    she met someplace—
      I never did get the hang of it
        but that's the gist.
  Thought more of them than she did
    of her old grandpop, I guess,"
    he'll chuckle
But he won't feel chuckley inside
  and it'll hurt a little then
And it'd hurt forever after
  when he drags out the snapshots
    he's sure to make of the gala gathering

"Yep, we were all together that year—
  except Martha and her gang in Germany—
  and, oh yes, Alice was gone—
  Mom, do you remember what it was
    about Alice that year?"
He'll squint across the room at Grandma
She'll remember all right
  and she'll tell him
    and then he'll remember too
      and hurt again
      and say
"Well—"
  and he'll clear his throat
    and talk about something else
Why, God, it'd be a sore place
  the rest of his life
Lord
  help Alice to see
  we rejoice in her new friends
  but this year
    let her let love in the family
      come first
Thank you
  Lord

IS FAIRNESS AN OBSOLETE WORD?

Dear God
  why does my younger sister
    get more privileges than me?
And why do Mama and Daddy
  let her get by
    with things that I
      would never dream of doing?
      Or if I did
        I'd be severely punished?
Why do I pay
  for my horse's feed
    out of my paper-route money
  and she gets to charge her stuff
    to Daddy's account
      everywhere she goes?
It's just not fair!
And she can call me stupid
  or sweetie
  or say, "Shut up, Punk"
    in that nasty tone of voice
  where Mama can hear her
    and so can Daddy
  and they act like they're deaf
But if I so much as whisper such stuff
  Daddy gets mad
  and Mama goes into a
    be-quiet-Dino mood
It makes me wonder
  Is fairness an obsolete word?
I remember a family discussion
  about three years ago
    where we all decided
      that any kid
        could stay up till eleven
          when they finally got in the tenth grade
Well, I'm in the tenth grade now

but do you think they'll let ME stay up?
Not on your life
I'm still sent packing off at ten
  with the excuse that I'm a paper boy
  and papers have to be delivered early
Just this morning
  Mama had said
    "A promise is a promise"
      when I tried to get out of going out
        collecting from my customers
I had a good reason
  It was raining
    and I had just been sick
But I had to go anyway
Then tonight
  my cousins came to see me
    and one of them
      wanted to ride our tandem bike with me
The sky was clear
  and the stars shone bright
but I couldn't go
You might get wet, Dino
Mama said
And we don't want you to get sick
But what about this morning, God
Didn't she care if I got sick then?
God, how can I make them fair?

Lord, a promise IS a promise
  and I know example teaches better
    than reminding ever can
Thanks for letting me be reminded
I'll tell the boy tomorrow
  "New bedtime—eleven o'clock!"
and watch his eyes light up
Only, Lord

you'll have to help him—
Let the less than seven hours be sleep enough
  to keep his mind alert in school
  to keep his body strong
And on these other complaints, Jesus
  (my, there are a lot of them)
  help him to understand
    that fairness
      doesn't mean treating everybody alike
        in everything
      (he wouldn't want that, really)
but fairness is
  giving each one
    what he seems to need the most
Lord
  help me to be fair
and help me as a mother
  to be willing
    to see things through a child's eyes
      more often
  that they might all know—
    especially Dino—
  that they're all loved much
    in special ways
but the accounts can never balance
  exactly
because love can't be measured out by cupfuls
and love is all of worth I have to give

God
  thank you
    for showing my mother
      wisdom
        and
      fairness
I'm glad that she

now lets me
  go to bed at eleven
I really am grateful
  but why can't she see
    that my sister
      who is not yet in the tenth grade
    should wait her turn
      instead of already
        getting to stay up till eleven?
That's not fair
  letting her off
  not making her wait
    like I had to do
Thank you
  God

Rivalry
  minding other people's business
Lord
  it's inborn
    in most of us
  isn't it?
Often
  I've been engaged
    in a labor of love
      and spoiled it
        by resentment
      when I've spotted someone else
        being lazy
        doing HIS thing
Even Peter rivaled
  and it kept him
    from being satisfied
      in the very presence
        of the Living Lord
When he'd professed

       unending love
          three times
Peter had to spoil it
   pointing to John
   asking
       Lord, what about him?
And Jesus
   gentle Jesus
       had to reprove him
          Peter, that's not your business
          Peter, follow me
          Peter, be satisfied
             with the portion
                I have chosen
                   especially for you
Lord
   help Dino to see
       how "Follow thou me" applies to him
   let Dino be delighted
       with the portion
          that pleases him for himself
             and not look to see
                how it stacks up
                   alongside another's portion
And Lord
   keep on saying
       Irene, what is that to thee?
       Follow thou me
   as often as I need to hear it
Lord, you're getting through . . .

SPECIAL PRIVILEGES

Lord
  why is it
    that special privileges
      backfire
        more often than not?
It really was a sacrifice
  for all the rest of us
    to let one daughter spend
      that extra week at the beach
        after she'd already been gone
          most of the summer
          having fun
        while the rest of us
          did our chores
          and hers
(it takes everybody's all-the-time-help
  to keep a big family going)
But we were unanimously
  tickled
    to give her the present
      of the extra fun week
And the surprised thank-you letter
  she wrote us
    was overwhelmingly full of love
    and I'll-be-grateful-forever-after-ness
I guess that's why
  I was caught so off-guard
    when on her second day at home
      she complained so loudly
        and so peevishly
      at having to baby-sit for such long hours
      with our little ones
Why, I'd have thought
  her thank you
    acted out
    would have lasted

>   the rest of the summer
>   instead of barely a day
> But no
>   the snarling began at once
>   grew to crescendo promptly
>   and hasn't yet subsided
> Why even when she's not being asked to help
>   she growls in retrospect
> She's special to me
>   all the children are
> And I just plain
>   don't understand this in her
> Can you help me try?

THE DATING GAME

Lord
  my birthday is in two months
    and I'll be seventeen
but Mom still won't let me go
  to the football game
    with a member of the opposite sex
I don't know what she thinks will happen
Maybe she thinks if I'm dating this year
  I'll be married and have a family next year
It makes me wonder how she acted on her dates
  when she was young
She knows I'm not going to do anything bad
  doesn't she?
My best friend
  —Mama thinks she's such a peach—
  has been dating ever since she was fourteen
    and I haven't noticed any ill effects in her
  She wouldn't dream of going off
    and getting married
    or anything like that
Lord
  why couldn't I go?

Lord
  about this car dating to games
    nearly an hour's ride away—
The highway at night
  is SO treacherous
And part of the way
  is on "killer highway 301"
(it's earned the name)
And besides
  the racial incidents
  after some of these games
  in our newly HEW'd world
    have been frightening—
  rocks thrown at buses

mobs fighting on the field
  police officers called to settle a fracas—
The whole thing is scary to me
  Jesus
I cringe at their going
  to away-from-home games at all
and then she comes up
  wanting to go to one
    on her very first single date
(I've not known her to have
  a double date even before)
"And, by the way," I asked her
  "Who is this Freddy fellow anyhow?
  Do you have his picture?"
    (her billfold's always bulging)
  "Is he on dope or anything?" I asked
    only half-joking
The kids all jeered

> *Freddy on dope?*
> *Mom, you've got to be kidding!*
> *Freddy takes PIANO LESSONS!*

My too-male-for-that son
  guffawed in derision
  (at me, not at Freddy
    Freddy's A-okay in his book)
His picture looked short-haired
  bespectacled
    positively harmless
but how could I know what kind of driver he was?
It was so much easier to say no
  to put off a little longer
    her fledgling flight into womanhood
      (to let her wait until MY wings were stronger)
  and so we decided
    her daddy and I

that since her older brother
   hadn't really started dating
      until Christmas of his senior year
   it would be well enough
      for her to wait, too
I wasn't thinking
   just of her
      but of the precedent
         for the four younger siblings
            soon following after
We told her "No
   no single dating till after Christmas
      till when you're seventeen"
Well, she sputtered
   but just a little
and I had a notion
   —I still do—
that subconsciously
   she was secretly pleased
      at having such gauche
         such fuddy-duddy folks
      who made such a to-do
         at her growing up
         at her coming of age
            whatever that means
She went to the game anyhow
   and had a good time
      judging from her hoarseness the next day
and it WAS a halfway date after all
Freddy bought her ticket
   and sat beside her on the bus
God
   the world's whirling so fast
      that my mind whirls too
         and leaps ahead
When she says

Can I go to the game with Freddy?
I translate it into
Mama, I wanna get married
and that's not what she means at all
I know there are disadvantages
   to beginning to date too late
   as well as too soon
Lord
   help us to discern
      the right pattern for OUR children
         and cleave to it
      no matter what anyone else does
and help me
   Lord
      with every decision
         to bring our daughters up
      to be ready to face
         what life will bring to them
and
   Lord
   take my foot off the brake
      when you're ready
         for them to fly

HIGHER EDUCATION

I felt like crawling into a corner
  and licking my wounds, Lord
    You know I did
    no point in pretending otherwise
We'd all been
  looking forward so eagerly
    to the first coming home
      of our first collegiate son
and we were brimming with questions
  me especially
about courses and profs and roommates
  and chow halls
But when he walked in
  all tall and handsome
    and wearing an air of
      I'm grown up now
      Please don't touch me
  he shoved us aside
    hardly saying hello
      and closeted himself
        with the telephone
        letting it rest
          caressingly
        on his shoulder
      while he poured out his soul
        lengthily
      to his girl friend
The rest of us
  who were only paying the bills
    right and left
    working late hours for the wherewithal
    (yes, all the ugliness of self-pity
      and martyrdom
        crept in)
we were left standing

with our faces hanging out
Jesus
   you know it's not that I'm jealous
     of his friends
        I love 'em too—especially his girl
   But how come
     Lord?
How come kids can be so unfeeling
   so discourteous as all that?
Oh, I'll recover
   (I have already as a matter of fact
     and from several other blows, too
        like the afternoon he walked in the next time
          —as expected and deliciously anticipated—
       sniffed the feast I'd slaved all day preparing
         in his honor
       and announced that he and his girl
         would be eating out—
           at some hamburger joint)
What I want to know
   Lord
     is how to make him sensitive
       to the feelings of others
       not just to his own selfish druthers
     so that other people won't find themselves
       forever having to make allowances for him
       forever having to overlook his actions
         and love him in spite of himself
What it boils down to, Lord
   is, How can I bring him up right
     now that he's already grown?
   how can I make him
     as willing to give
       as he is to receive
         at this late date?

And maybe
  while you're at it
Lord
   maybe I need
     some instructions
       along that line
     myself

FRAGILE—HANDLE WITH CARE

Lord
  his instructions
    for taking care of
      his new ten-speed bike
  were SO meticulous
He posted them in his room
  and required almost
    a signature in blood
      of anyone who asked to borrow it
        to try it out
          to touch it even
The list is there still:

People who have my permission
  to use my ten-speed
    (not valid if otherwise stated)
  Tommy
  Jimmy
  Dino
  Sue
  Eddie
After use
  bring my bike up to my room
    [a second-story room, mind you]
    lean against closet doors
    and wipe off the whole bike
      with the towel on my desk
        [probably one of the beautiful terry ones
          my mother sent for Christmas]
Pay special attention
  to the sprockets
    and the back derailer
      to remove all dust and sand

You know where the bike is now, Lord
  and has been for days
Out in the backyard

leaning against a tree
      dripping from our daily showers
From the look of it
   where the raindrops didn't hit
      it hasn't been toweled for centuries
The sprockets and back derailer
   especially
      show signs of criminal neglect
Dust and dirt and sand
   have set in
      with a ninety-year lease
It's as if he's lost his former love
   already
He'd probably be surprised
   if I reminded him about the list
      and what good care he pledged himself
         to take of it forever
* * * * * * * * * * * * *
How's that, Lord?
   What are you asking me?
Oh yes
   I confess
      I'd probably be surprised too
         to be reminded of my gifts from you
            that I had pledged myself
               to treasure
               to keep pristine forever
                  by paying careful attention
                  to who was with them
                  and how they were cared for
Why, some days
   I'm so neglectful
      YOU must wonder if *I* care
Lord
   I do care
Make me eternally mindful

FAT HEAD

Lord
  I'm not pretending to be
    just the right size
      or anything like that
but this son of mine
  who's forever bugging me
    about my weight—
Take care of him, Lord
I can see
  that he may be
    eventually
  of elephantine proportions
Not because he shows any
  tendency
    in that direction
but because he is so highly intolerant
  of those who do
He has something yet to learn
  about acceptance of others
    exactly as they are
      without condemnation
      without if-only reservation
Oh, Lord
  we all have so much to learn
    above loving
    and not judging
Lord
  I know you can teach us
    fat or thin
I know that if we feed on
  your sweetness
    we'll all become
      precisely the right size
      for your glory
Oh, give that son to know

that every sin not manifested in his flesh
   is not absent by his goodness
      but by your mercy
Don't make him learn it
   the hard way

SIGNS OF SPRING

A fluttery coupling of birds
  in instinctual embrace
    on the grass
      beside the sidewalk
A black and white sandwich of cats
  locked in brazen copulation
  on the concrete driveway
    in broad daylight
Fragrant
  delicate
    fragile
      flowers
        poking through everywhere
And some boy's class ring
  on the finger
    of my teen-age daughter
O Lord
  you know how much I love
    the usual signs of spring
      the ones that poets have extolled
        and raved about
And I'm glad to be
  newly aware
    that you have made everything beautiful
      in its time
    even my daughter
But Lord
  it's hard to accept
    having some special boy
      single her out
        for some special notice
      so soon
How can I handle that, Lord,
Why
  she's only a little girl
  for all her blossoming

I want SO
   to keep her a little girl
      a tiny while longer
She's got years and years
   to be a femme fatale
The boy?
Oh Lord
   You know I like him just fine
      love him, really
Why
   perhaps
      he's the very one
         I'd pick out for her
      if I was doing the choosing
BUT NOT YET, LORD
Lord
   she's so young
   he's so young
      to be serious
Please, Lord
   can't you make them wait
      until I grow up?

ON NECK-WRINGING

"I'm gonna wring Tommy's neck!"
Lord
  You know I said it loud
    and I meant it loud
As the world sees things
  I was absolutely justified
    had all the right on my side
Imagine!
As old as he is
  to come in
    and unload
      all my still wet laundry
        from the dryer
      so he could expedite the drying
      of what he needed
        right now
Oh
  that was all right
It wouldn't have mattered a bit
But what did he do
  with all the still wet clothes
    when his own were dry?
Did he put them back in the dryer
  and set it to spinning
    so the rest of us
      would have what we needed
        later?
Oh no
  not him
He had glopped all our stuff
  wrinkly and wet
    on the top of the washer
      and there it sat
The dryer agape

   empty
   ajar
Tommy had what HE wanted
To heck with the rest of us
And Lord
   that wasn't unusual
      it was typical
He's unbelievably inconsiderate and selfish
   Lord
Why
   I don't even have to ask
      to see if Tommy's come home
I can just check the bathroom sink
If it's festooned
   with lots of longish dark hair
      Tommy's been here
If the scoured-white-that-morning sink
   is smudged greasy gray
      Tommy's been there
If the carport's strewn
   with insulation
   sawdust
   nails
   and wire
      Tommy's been
Why
   when he takes a shower
      you'd think no one else
         in the family
      would ever want any hot water
         he lets it run so long
   and when he takes the soaking kind of bath
      the ring he always leaves
         —his inimitable calling card—
      is ABOVE the overflow
         and a sodden washrag

garnishes the tub's rim
And presents?
  Oh, he's perfectly delighted
    when someone gives him something
      but generosity is not
        his middle name
Lord
  how could I have made
    such an absolute mess of him
      when I've had
        such good-looking
        intelligent
          raw material
            to work with
              for twenty years?
I confess I've heard
  similar laments
    from the lips of other
      well-meaning mothers
It's as if some kids
  are ten-speed bikes
    with gears
      for everything except
        being considerate

* * * * * * * * *

Thank you, Lord
  for taking my despair
    and anger
  and giving me
    understanding and light
      beyond what I'd had before
Yes
  I see
    that I've been expecting
      instant maturity
Twenty years

isn't really long
   at all
You've called to mind
   some of my recent selfish inconsiderateness
      though I'm two score
         and more
Tommy's sins
   and mine
      are not deliberate meanness
      calculated contrariness
      engineered inconsiderateness
but inevitabilities
   of our self-centered lives
Lord
   I see the answer
      doesn't lie
         in picking up the pieces
         in disciplined doing
      but in transformation of our centeredness
         from serving self
            to letting you
               exist in us
                  through us
                  for us
Lord
so surround us
   and all our doings
that our lives
   will exemplify
      you
And Lord
don't let us settle
   for anything less

HELPMEET

I feel sorry
  for whoever turns out
    to be his wife, Lord
Will her love last?
Or will it turn to something else
  when she's had it up to here
    with waiting on him hand and foot
    cleaning up after him forever
      with no hint of reciprocity or gratitude
      but an overbearing air
        of *"I'm entitled"*
Lord
  you've got to set him straight
    before too late
Thank you, Lord
  that nothing is impossible with you
  that miracles are your everyday gift
    to those who need them
  that you can do
    in the twinkling of an eye
      what all my efforts
        for twenty years
          have strived in vain about
I'm glad we all keep on
  needing your help
    Lord
because with your help
  with your gifts
you invariably
  give
    yourself
Thank you, Lord
I'm glad that you come with the package

DRIVER'S LICENSE DREAD

Lord
  you know how it worried me
    (forgive my pretending "Let not your heart
    be troubled" was only for funerals)
    when our kids
      crept close to being
        old enough to drive
I want to thank you now
  several years later
    that you've kept them careful
      safety conscious
        (they've even made
          a seat-belter
            out of me!)
    that you've made them
      such willing and handy and excellent
      errand runners
And most of all, Lord
  thank you that you've let them learn
    to pray your blessing
      on every journey
Lord
  I'm glad you let them drive
    when I was still unwilling
Lord
  keep on keeping them safe
Keep on keeping them
  counting on you

REPORT CARD REPORTING

It was a truly s
u
b
t
e
r
r
a
n
e
a
n

r
e
p
o
r
t

c
a
r
d
  Lord
Why
  he must have had to dig a hole
    to sink that low
Just looking at it
  put me in such a state of shock
    I shoved it somewhere
      out of sight
    and couldn't even find it
      for several weeks thereafter
It was out of sight
  all right
    but hardly out of my mind
How'd it strike you, Lord?
  One D

and all the rest E's
   (they don't stand for excellent
      in our school)
It just plain struck me
What a blow!
I couldn't even talk to him about it
   couldn't believe it, really
And so I wrote a note
   (you saw it
      and the hurt in my heart)
"Dear Dino
   I don't want to know
      how it happened
   I just want you
      to write down
         how you feel about it
            and
         what you think
            we ought to do about it
   Or would you rather
      just quit school?"

*"Since you don't want to know
   how it happened
      I won't tell you
I will tell you
   how I feel about it
      in a minute
But first
   let me explain"*

His explanation
   (what I thought I didn't want)
      was rather lengthy
         wasn't it, Lord?
   All about a teacher
      who didn't know her stuff

and one who did
   but hadn't gotten through to him
and about a subject
   that fascinates him
   and the teacher is okay
   and it's really easy
   but he hadn't studied
and another still
   where he thinks the teacher goofed
     in figuring his grade
Well, all of that
   sounded like excuses—
     honest reasons as he saw it
I nodded my understanding as I read
   the explanation I didn't want
     of things I couldn't do anything about
But what came next, Lord
   I needed to hear
   It socked me into awareness
     of something I'd never considered
     before

"You and Daddy
  made a bad mistake
    in always telling us
      how smart we are
You should not have said that
But I am sure
  that if you will require me
    to really study
      at least an hour each night
  and let me stay after school in Spanish
    for a while
  I will do very good
    [my grammar winced]
    next time

I am sorry
  to dissapoint you"
  [my spelling turned a somersault]

Lord
  did we make a bad mistake
    in praising this child?
Has acknowledging his inborn ability
  been altogether wrong
  made him expect achievement
    without effort
    and headed him down the wrong road
      too long?
What was wrong to start with, Lord?
Shouldn't pride of accomplishment
  built-in stick-to-it-ive-ness
    have been nurtured already
      to some kind of maturity
        by the eleventh grade
      and not require
        an ever-zealous Mama accelerator
          to keep it in motion?
And why is it, Lord
  that MY good resolves
    dissolve
      almost instantly I make them?
I surely meant
  to follow his suggestions
  and make him work
and I did
  for a little while
    and then succumbed
      to his immediate druthers
        letting him
          do
          this or that

             letting him
                  go
             here and there
without making him study first
Lord
  I flubbed it
    along with him
Lord
  you know best
Please take over
* * * * * * * * * * * * *
It's weeks later, Lord
At last reporting
  there was that unexpected
    unbelievable
    miraculous
       A in English
       (a skyrocketing success
          because they're on science fiction
          and he's an expert's expert on that
            and has been for years)
  and some lesser inching up
    in SOME other subjects
      but not in all
and I see other
  more significant things
    happening in his ilfe
Joking about grades the other day
  he laughingly announced
    Oh, I've quit thinking about grades
    I'm going to be a religious fanatic
I know
  those two don't have to be
    mutually exclusive, Lord
But if they did
  I'm glad you've given him

    to choose the better part
    and that there's evidence already
      that he's not joking
    but that you're using him
      to witness
        to your reality
Once upon a time
  when *I* was a fanatic
    not, forgive me, for you
    but for, forgive me, straight A's
      the Phi Beta Kappa, summa-cum-laude bit
  I thought THAT was all there was
    mutually exclusive of everything else
      including you
  Why
    at his age
      I didn't even know
        that you were an option
Thank you, Lord
  for getting Dino's priorities
    so soundly grounded
Thank you
  that he's had sense enough to choose you
    over all the acclaim
      the world has to offer
Thanks for becoming
  the chosen center of his life
    so early
Oh, Lord
  grow in him
    and let him grow
      in you

SUNNY SIDE UP?

Like Wow, Lord!
  I mean
    just how persnickety
      can one person get?
How finicky
  should I have to put up with?
She's a fantastic kid, Lord
  fascinating
You've never made another one like her
  and I love to please her
    but really—
"Here you are, Susan
  I know you've got to where
    you don't care
      for scrambled eggs
        or fried
        or poached
        or in French toast
      so I boiled a couple
        for YOUR breakfast
"They're nice and hot
  and good and hard—
    just the way you like them"
I handed her the bowl
  with the two ready-for-enjoying
    pretty brown eggs
  feeling rather righteous
    that I'd been ambitious enough
      to fix a variety of breakfasts
        and satisfy everybody's appetite
But Susan's voice was hurt
  quavery
    anything but satisfied

Don't we have any white eggs, Mama?
I can't eat the brown ones

Lord
  I nearly toppled
I looked my incredulity straight at her
  "Can you tell the difference
    once they're peeled?
  Surely, Susan
    you've got to be kidding"
But she was dead serious

I'm sorry, Mama
  but I just don't care
    for brown eggs anymore
They just don't taste the same

You know, Lord
  I might have understood
    a faint preference
      by a professional connoisseur
      or a full-time gourmet
but for white eggs to be delicious
  and brown ones inedible
No, Lord
  I couldn't understand that
  I thought it was the limit
But I had something still to learn
  didn't I?
The next day
  she was almost late for school
  and told me why

I had to wait for Tommy to get out of the bathroom
so I could brush my teeth

"But couldn't you have used
  the other upstairs bathroom?
    I know it was empty"
      (I wouldn't have had the effrontery
        to suggest she use

        the downstairs one
        or the kitchen sink
        or a glass of water
          in the backyard
          and spit on the grass)
Her indignation surfaced
  as if anyone should know
    the answer to THAT stupid question

No
  of course not
I couldn't brush my teeth in that one
because the faucet turns the other way
"The what?"
  I shook my head to clear the cobwebs
  I had been working kind of hard
Lord
  I thought I heard her wrong
But I had heard her right
  from the start
Let me explain
  as she explained to me:
See
  the upstairs bathrooms
    are back to back
    (plumbing's cheaper like that)
    the door of one
      being to the right of the sink
    the door of the other
      being to the left of the sink
    and if a righthanded person
      brushes her teeth
        in the bathroom with the door
          to the right of the sink
      and doesn't happen to shut the door
        quite all the way

      she just might bump her elbow
The faucet turns the other way
See?
  I do

* * * * * * * * * * * * *

Logic
  I love you
Understanding
  you're indispensable
Adaptability?
  some days you're a long way off
    invisible beyond some distant horizon
Lord
  I thank you
    that necessity
      is the mother of many things
        —even adaptability maybe
    and that last year
      at summer camp
        according to her letter home
      Susan got so hungry
        she even ate second·helpings
          of SCRAMBLED EGGS!
            (I wonder what color their shells
              were—
            she didn't seem to know)
        and she probably brushed her teeth
          accepting whatever facilities they had
Oh, Lord
  we do all have preferences
    even I
  and logical reasons for them
    satisfactory to ourselves
  and I'm really delighted
    that you've made our children
      so discriminating

    so unique
    so interestingly finicky
and that you do
  let them be adaptable
    when it's absolutely necessary
But Lord
  make all of us
    who have eaten what we wanted
      and brushed our teeth so fastidiously—
  make us
    alively and responsively
      aware of those
        whose hunger scours city streets
          for any feast of garbage
        whose faucets don't turn on at all
          except to empty air
Lord
  help us
    to grow up

SURPRISED BY JOY

God
  I really am thankful
    that you gave me parents
      and a home
      and a brother
      and sisters
      and such a good life
    and I thank you
      for many other things
        that your goodness has given me
Sure
  my parents
    are almost
      the strictest in town
        and as sheltering of their kids
          as
          a mama cat with baby kittens
            or
          parent birds
            with newly hatched nestlings
As you know
  when I asked my folks
    if I could go
      on a car rally
    I was set to argue
      about it
      because of the firm
        decisive
          "No"
        that I expected
But for some reason
  unknown to me
    they said
      Sure, son, you can go
and they even let me go
  a second time

>   *to an eastern state rally*
>   *as well as to a race in Virginia*
>   *with my explorer post*
> *As I said*
>   *I don't know why*
>   *I still can't believe it*
>   *I almost keep expecting*
>   *them to change their minds*
>   *and make it retroactive somehow*
>   *If I didn't have the trophy*
>   *(we came in second place)*
>   *to prove it*
>   *I'd have to keep on*
>   *pinching myself*
>   *to see if it was so*
> *Anyway*
>   *thanks*
>   *God*
>   *for letting them see things*
>   *from my point of view*
>   *for once*
> *And God*
>   *do you suppose*
>   *you can make it happen*
>   *again*
>   *sometime?*
> *Please?*

CONCLUSION LEAPING
WITH TRAP RUNNING

We had taken
  kind of a new acquaintance
    with deep needs
    to a lit-up meeting
      the kind where people think
        Jesus is still for real
He had seeeemed
  to me
    stand-offish
    unresponsive
      as I kept watch
        from the corner of my eye
And when we dropped him off
  at his house
    and returned to our own
I was rehashing
  my disappointment
    that he hadn't been moved
      to some kind of commitment

Mama!

I was interrupted
  mercifully
before I consigned him
  to hopeless oblivion
forever
Our son explained
  with an intuition and wisdom
    putting my own to shame

Mama
  Henry was just gonna sit
    and listen
    and find out what happens
      over there
    before he started making

>   *enough noise of his own*
>   *that he couldn't tell*

I got the hint
  that I'd be smart
    to follow his example
      instead of sounding off so
Oh, Lord
  the boy is right
Forgive me
  that I so often begin my noise
    and my silent inward judgments
      so soon
    that I never find out what's happening
      and maybe even stop anything
        FROM happening
Give me the patience
  that can let a wound heal
    instead of forever prodding
      and probing
    and scratching scabs off
      and keeping wounds raw
Let me relax
  and trust you to take care of
    what I've put in your hands

OFF

Lord
  I'm 100 percent
    absolutely
  sick and tired of it
We've had a rule for years
  NO GOING OFF WITHOUT PERMISSION
  I ALWAYS NEED TO KNOW
    WHERE YOU ARE
He knows it very well
He could recite it perfectly
So why does he
  evaporate like this
  just suddenly disappear
    without warning
    and stay gone for hours?
I haven't the faintest idea
  where to find him
We've hollered in every direction
  telephoned the friends we could think of
Nobody's seen him, Lord
At this point
  I'm aggravated
    disgusted
  not so much wondering
    WHERE he is
      as
    WHY he is
      someplace
      anyplace
    in flagrant violation
      of our very well-taught rule
        of such long standing
There's just no sense in it, Lord
You know how I hate violence
  especially in me

  but I'm churning with it
   just now
I want to see him punished
 made thoroughly repentant
  for willfully taking off
I'll not have an ounce of sympathy
 when he shows up
not after the turmoil and frustration
 he's put me through
I don't even want to love him, Lord
Every instinct tells me
 I'm entitled
  to be mad as hell
And Lord
 I am
He's absolutely ruined with distress
 what should have been a pleasant evening
It's surely such as this
 that makes parents gray-headed
  dead with heart attacks
  attacked with ulcers
   riddled with arthritis
    alienated from you—
Oh Lord
 that last one—
 that's what it's all about
  isn't it?
And I'll keep on having situations that bug me
 as long as I will let the enemy
  use them
   to separate me from you
Lord
 somehow
  get through to me
   again and again

Let me praise you
   for everything
Lord
   thank you
      that Dino's gone off
         without permission
Use this trespass to your glory

To God
I'm only seventeen
   and six feet tall
   and so helpless
that I can't
   go out of the yard
      without permission
I must stay
   at home
   and play in my sandbox
      in the backyard
I went to a friend's
   a block away
      and stayed one hour
         which seemed an eternity
            to my worrying mother
She lets on
   how exasperated
      she is
         to have her seventeen-year-old son
            temporarily away from his sandbox
But my sister gets gone
   for hours on her horse
      five or ten blocks away
   without permission of course
      and for at least three hours
My mother isn't worried
   and/or doesn't fuss at

>   *her fifteen-year-old daughter*
>   *even one little bit*
> Lord
>   *why don't parents be fair*
>   *and at least listen a little*
>   *and not worry about a seventeen-year-old son*
>   *temporarily out of place?*
> *I could say more*
>   *but I won't*
> *Show 'em, please?*

Oh, thank you, Lord
   that you're really answering prayers
      you're really opening eyes
         with this one
My eyes, Lord
Thanks for showing me
   that I need to update the rule
      to show it isn't meant
         to tie anyone to an apron string
It's not really about permissions
   any longer
      is it?
And hasn't been for some time
But because I hadn't changed the phrasing
   he naturally thought it was
      and naturally resented it
So
   he knows
      that when he comes home from school
         and I'm not here
      he can count on a note
on the cookie jar on the table
   or on the front of the refrigerator
      telling where I've gone
      and when I plan to be back

just so he'll know
     that's all
And Lord
  that's what I still want from him
    so I'll know
      that's all
Thank you, Lord
  that he doesn't need permission anymore
We don't have such a rule
He is a big kid now
No more sandbox
  no more tiddledywinks
    no more *Mother, may I*
Just notification
  so I'll know
    and be knowledgeable
      when the phone rings for him
      or the friend stops by
      or I need him for something

THE LIVING END—AS A NEW BEGINNING

You knew, Lord
  that I had reached
    the absolute end
      of my rope
  that I was
    sick with despair
      over the contrariness
      of that little one
I'd paddled until my arm was weary
  threatened until my voice was gone
    prayed until my knees ached
      and cringed at every confrontation
But nothing
  but nothing
    was getting through
      to her
        or you
Unruliness
  disrespect
    downright insurgent rebellion
      were every moment emanating
Lord
  would we survive?
I really wondered
Oh, how I marvel at your timing
  its intricate precision
      never a second too soon
      never a moment too late
      but exactly when we need you
      exactly
No, Lord
  I didn't get through to her
But when I despaired
  of doing anything except giving up
    and finally hushed
you

    who had been listening all along
you, Lord
   got through to me
Thank you, Lord
   for the just-right book arriving
      and the perfect opportunity to read it
   its teaching so clear
      so on-the-nose relevant:
   "Not an eye for an eye
      or a tooth for a tooth
      hostility for hostility
      violence for violence
But I say to you
   love for hate
   good for those who misuse you
   love everywhere
      Praise me
         for everything
            exactly as it is"
Exactly as it is?
Including an unreasonable
   obstreperous child, Lord?
"ESPECIALLY her
   because I am using her
      to teach you something
         you need to know
         something you must learn
            if you're to grow
            if you're to be
               of any use at all to me"
We heard
   and saw
      and began
         by your grace
            to follow your instructions:

"Love
  no matter what
Acceptance
  of the unacceptable"
And your miracle was immediate
  overnight
    a calming
    a soothing
    a loving
      response to love
And then
  lest we weaken
  lest we forget
  lest we be tempted
    to return to our old ineffectual
      making-things-worse ways
  you sent reinforcement
    through a sermon
      in someone else's church
    and got us there to hear it
      on Mother's Day
"Once a day
  every day
    all day" love
"Once a day
  every day
    all day" love
Thank you, Lord
  that it isn't always easy
Thank you, Lord
  that it's impossible
    without your help
But thank you, Lord
  that you do help
    abundantly

  above all we could ask or think
  when we offer you our willingness
We praise you, Lord
  for your infinite patience WITH us
  Your infinite patience IN us
    for others
Get us out of the way
  Lord
    so you can come through

READING GLASSES

Well, Lord
  if I'm to give thanks in everything
    I guess I'll have to thank you
      that I have to wear reading glasses now
      to make out all that fine print
      (funny how they started
        using fine print on everything
        the last year or so)
The visual needs
  of people my age
    are so inevitable
    so predictable
    so universal
      we can borrow one another's glasses
      and hardly notice the difference
        We can even order "prescription lenses"
        from a mail-order catalog
        with no other "prescription"
          than our sex and age
God
  maybe are you saying
    that at our age
      you want us to quit focusing
        on minor flaws in others
    that you want us to lean back
      at arm's length
      and take a divine perspective on things?
Are you maybe saying
  "Don't keep on being enslaved
    by the minutiae of life
  but see my grand plan"?
Yes
  thank you, Lord
    there are some things about vision
      I needed to know

Forgive me for my lifelong stubbornness
   my insisting that my way of looking at things
      was the right way
         the only way
Forgive me that I was too nearsighted
   for forty-odd years
Thank you, Lord
   for some indication
      that I'm getting more farsighted now
Thank you
   that you always give what is needful
And so let this new way of looking
   apply to my children, Lord
      so I won't keep on nit-picking
      but rejoice in how wonderful they are
         in spite of me

IF THERE BE ANYTHING LOVELY, THINK ABOUT IT

Lord
  forgive me
    that I so often
      pour out my complaints
        against the six special blessings
          you've given my husband and me
I seem to be in the habit
  of pouring out negatives
    asking for help
  instead of pouring out positives
    when you've provided it
      above all I could ask or think
So now
  for once
    just let me thank you
      for the six of them
        all together
        and every single one
For the handsomeness of a son
  his stretching tallness
  emerging from awkwardness
    into growing manhood
  so good-looking
    I have to avert my eyes
      not to be overwhelmed
For another son
  whose divine sense of justice
    is so high
      that he won't accept
        HIS HALF
          of a compromise
        unless he thinks
          the other guy's half
          is just as good
For a daughter

who yesterday, all unasked
  began to clear the dirty dishes
    from the table
  when I had unexpected guests
who works her way
  through much of school
    with scholarship tuition
    and odd-job lunch money
And for another daughter
  whose galloping pursuit
    of all that interests her
  keeps me agog at her energy
  and whose awareness of my needs
    to be loved
    to be understood
      is healing balm
And let me thank you
  for the unfolding miracle of language
  in our once-upon-a-time-deaf daughter
  the daily wonder of it
her
  Thank you, find it Dino's ball
  when I handed her what she had lost
    in the long grass
  might not be perfect language
    for an ordinary eight-year-old
      but she's super-ordinary
        to us
and I thank you for
  our adopted daughter
    the one you chose
      especially for us
    not, as we thought, because she needed us
      but because we needed her
        so very much

Thank you, Lord
  for each of them
  exactly as they are
that they are yours
      and that you know their needs
        and ours
  and will provide
    abundantly
      forever

SLOWPOKE

Forgive me, Lord
  that I've been forever
    so concerned about
      the pokiness of my son
        who seems to dawdle forever
          over everything
Thank you
  for letting me find out
    what he's been up to
      all along
I've thought he was such a lousy paper boy
  for all those people
    slow about deliveries
    forever about collections
    forgetful about his customers
    uncareful about the puddles
But then a woman called one day
  not to complain
    (they often did)
  not to say he'd forgotten her paper
    (we'd had plenty of calls like that)
    or that it got drenched in the rain
      (that always bugged 'em)
      or that he should have collected already
        (Sorry, Ma'am, I'll send him tomorrow)
  but just to express her appreciation
    for him
"Our two-and-a-half-year-old Tricia
  is crazy about your Dino"
    she gushed
"Yes"
  I acknowledged
    "little children
      always love him
        —for some reason"
"Why," she said
  "he's the sweetest thing

    I ever saw
When he comes to collect
    Tricia always wants to pay a penny
        and Dino takes the time
            to write out a full receipt for her
                in triplicate
            as well as one for me
    She puts it in her pocket
        and carries it around for days
            just thrilled to death"
Another day
    another woman called
        not to complain
            either
"Irene
    your Dino just gave our little Jamie
        a whole dollar
    when he saw him in the store
I thought I should tell you
    in case he wasn't supposed to do that
Jamie was tickled pink
He just loves Dino"
Well
    it was his money, Lord
and if he wanted to squander it
    on little kids
instead of hoarding paper-route profits
    that was his business
But he'd never get ahead like that
What with his hating to collect
    and his overflowing generosity
        he barely scraped together
            what he needed
                to pay his bill each month
I found myself
    sometimes

    having to subsidize
But then I'd remember
  times when I'd asked him
    to go to the store for milk
      or bread
      or something else
And I'd said
  "Wait a minute, Dino
    and I'll get you some money"
But he'd always waved me away
  as he banged out the door
    Oh, that's all right, Mom
    I have enough
And he'd buy the milk
  or whatever
    out of his pocket
      not saving for tomorrow
        or next week
      when he'd have to pay his bill
Whatever he has
  is still for others, Lord
    for whoever needs it
      just now
Lord
  forgive my nagging
    still ringing in my ears
  "Dino, get on with it"
And thank you
  that he heard it
    and heeded it
      in his own special way
Forgive that I've been so condemning
  of his unbusinesslikeness
    his pokiness
    his detours to watch
      a bird building a nest

        a caterpillar humping across the road
        a man paving a street
     his detours to help
        a kid change a bicycle tire
        an old lady empty her trash
        a middle-aged man shovel snow
           from his drive
Lord
  let him keep on
    with HIS kind of businesslikeness
      YOUR kind
  living his life preciously
    like a little child
  living as he goes along
    and not waiting until
      he gets everything else done first
      the way I so often do
Lord
  don't give up
keep on trying to teach me
  to live like that

SERVANT SERVICE

Lord
  you were there
    the morning Tommy blew a gasket
     because gremlins had guzzled
      the milk all gone
       the night before
     and his work pants
      were still in the clothes basket
      reeking
      when he wanted them
       ready to wear
You heard
  the fierce banging
    of drawers and doors
     faint echoes of
      the slamming frustration in his heart
You knew
  the guilt in my gizzard
You felt
  the lump in my throat
    at his condemnation
     of my lousy attention
      to his comfort
and I suspect
  you looked over my shoulder
    and guided me into truth
     as I wrote down words
      after he roared off

"Dear Thomas—
  You will be overwhelmed with delight
    to learn that the laundry service
     and the milk supply
    around this joint
     are about to be
      fantastically
      escalated

These two services have
  admittedly
  been poorly handled in the past
    by an incompetent
      unpaid
      volunteer
        with other things on her mind
Beginning now, however
  someone new
    will discharge these responsibilities
      in a truly superlative manner
Your interests are
  as close to his heart
    as to your own
He won't even think
  about anything else
    except pleasing you
You will never have cause for complaint
  against him
He will prove an excellent, dependable servant
Imagine!
  gallons and gallons of milk
    whenever you want it
  clean blue jeans galore
    all the time
I am
  so overwhelmed
    with exuberant joy
  at this new arrangement
    that I feel
      all hallelujah inside
Rejoice with me
Let it blow your mind!
Here's how this Garden-of-Eden setup
  will operate:
    1) every night

                the new servant
                    will check the milk supply
                if there's not enough
                    he will haste
                        to the store
                        to buy beaucoup
                    providing his own wheels!
                    furnishing his own wherewithal!
            2) every night
                    said servant
                        will also check
                            the laundry basket
                if anything of yours
                    rests therein
                        reeking of anything
                            less than roses
                        he will sweeten it
                            with washing
                                drying
                                ironing even
                                    if you like
You are assured of
    perfect service
        perpetually
No extra charge
And you know something?
    I didn't even have to fire
        the old servant
            for her general incompetence
        she just up and quit
            announcing that twenty years
                was long enough
                    to have served
                        unthanked
                        unpaid
                        unappreciated

>   taken for granted
>   unremembered even on Mother's Day
>   (she must have gotten mixed up
>   in some of this deplorable
>   woman's lib stuff)
>   Just one thing more:
>   the name of the new servant
>   the epitome of efficiency
>   the paragon of perfection
>   His name is Tommy
>   Your name is Tommy?
>   Why
>   yes
>   who would have guessed
>   Of course
>   it's you
>   You're it
>   Congratulations!"

I do thank you, Lord
  for setting him free
  and me
  for showing us
    how wrong I've been
      thinking that a good mother
        did everything for her kids
You've opened my eyes
  to the truth
    that a good mother
      lets kids learn
        to do for themselves
She LETS them
  grow up
Thanks, Lord